Jeff Gordon

Jeff Gordon

Michael Bradley

BENCHMARK BOOKS

MARSHALL CAVENDISH
NEW YORK

Benchmark Books
Marshall Cavendish
99 White Plains Road
Tarrytown, NY 10591-9001
www.marshallcavendish.com

Library of Congress Cataloging-in-Publication Data

Bradley, Michael, 1962-
Jeff Gordon / by Michael Bradley.
p. cm. — (Benchmark all-stars)
Summary: A biography of the NASCAR driver, focusing on his triumphant
wins and disappointing losses.
Includes bibliographical references and index.
 ISBN 0-7614-1627-7
1. Gordon, Jeff, 1971—-Juvenile literature. 2. Automobile racing
drivers—United States—Biography—Juvenile literature. [1. Gordon,
Jeff, 1971- 2. Automobile racing drivers.] I. Title. II. Series.

GV1032.G67B73 2004
796.72'092--dc21

2003001416

Series design by Becky Terhune

Printed in Italy
1 3 5 6 4 2

Contents

A familiar sight—Jeff Gordon celebrates yet
another big win on the Winston Cup circuit.

CHAPTER ONE

Back on Top

The turnaround was tremendous. Jeff Gordon's last two *NASCAR* racing seasons—1999 and 2000—had been miserable. The start of 2001 had been tragic. But on a November 2001 afternoon at Atlanta Motor Speedway, Gordon was back on top.

The man who race fans loved—or loved to hate—won his fourth *Winston Cup* points title. Many had thought the driver in the multicolored number 24 Chevrolet Monte Carlo was finished—they were wrong. Gordon had overcome several changes in his team and fought off a slump that many other racers would have called a successful stretch.

It was good to be the best again. "I'm never one to say who's the greatest," Gordon said after winning the championship. "Every given weekend, there is another guy who is the best. It doesn't matter to me who is the greatest. As long as I'm winning and a part of a race team like this, you can call me the worst driver out there, and that's fine by me."

Nobody would ever dream of calling Jeff Gordon the worst. During his ten-year career on the NASCAR circuit, Gordon has accomplished more than almost any other driver. In the 2001 season he had won fifty-eight races and earned more than $70 million in prize

Gordon's multicolored car and his continued success have earned him the nickname "Rainbow Warrior."

money. His four Winston Cup titles (given to the season's top points earner) are third behind legends Richard Petty and Dale Earnhardt, who each have seven wins. The Winston Cup Series includes all NASCAR races held during a season. Drivers earn points for their finishes, and the one who finishes the year with the most points wins the championship.

Gordon's success has made him rich and given him rock-star status among NASCAR's loyal fans. At age thirty-three he has accomplished enough for two or three careers. And yet, he is just beginning. *Stock car* racing is usually the business of men in their thirties and forties. But Gordon became a superstar while still a young man. With so much success already behind him, one can only imagine what lies ahead.

"I've accomplished more than I ever could have

> **"It doesn't matter to me who is the greatest. As long as I'm winning and a part of a race team like this, you can call me the worst driver out there, and that's fine by me."**
> **—Jeff Gordon**

All NASCAR racers have fans, but few can boast as huge and loyal a group of supporters as Jeff Gordon can.

dreamed of," Gordon said. "I want to make a mark in this sport. I want to be in it for a long time."

It's no surprise Jeff Gordon has been successful in the big leagues. Ever since he was bombing around dirt tracks on his BMX bike as a child, he has loved speed. He was racing cars before he even had his driver's license. When he made his NASCAR debut at

Gordon's success has helped him become a celebrity. Here, he poses with late-night television star Jay Leno.

twenty-one, many wondered whether he would be able to handle the pressure and danger. But Gordon never doubted himself. Though he stands only 5′ 7″ (170 cm) tall, Gordon is a giant in his sport.

"Jeff is definitely in the group of the greatest drivers who have ever come along, if not the greatest," says Gordon's crew chief, Robbie Loomis. That doesn't mean Gordon is the most popular driver among the NASCAR set. He does have his share of loyal supporters, but his quick success has angered some of the sport's older fans. When his name is announced before races, there are just as many boos as cheers. He is called the "Rainbow

Warrior" because his car features so many vivid colors. Some fans prefer their drivers to be tougher and meaner.

Anybody who has tried to pass Gordon on a turn has learned how tough he is in the car. But his quick smile and squeaky-clean image—not to mention all those wins—don't appeal to everyone. Whether or not he is liked, Gordon's accomplishments have earned him the respect of many.

"Gordon's [greatness] is good for the whole racing fraternity," says Richard Petty, whose 200 career wins are by far the most ever. "You have to have a lead dog. You have to have someone out front for everyone else to shoot for."

Gordon has had plenty of success during his career. It has helped him become the kind of celebrity that companies want to hire to help sell their products. In 2001 he went to the Academy Awards and was invited to many of the exclusive parties held afterward. But it hasn't always been easy. As Petty says, Gordon is the one everybody wants to beat. And though he struggled for two seasons, he came back in 2001 with a magical season that included wins in six races and a return to the top of the NASCAR heap. It was another great chapter in a great racing life.

And there's plenty more to come.

Jeff Gordon takes a moment to relax during a practice race prior to the Daytona 500 in February 2000.

CHAPTER TWO

Getting Started

Jeff Gordon was born to drive. Born in Vallejo, California, on August 4, 1971, Jeff was four when he started racing. Back then, instead of cars, he pedaled BMX bikes. That ended quickly, when his mother, Carol Bickford, decided it was too dangerous. "At BMX events, they were hauling kids away in ambulances all the time," Carol said. Jeff needed something safer, so his stepfather, John Bickford, bought Jeff his first car, a *quarter midget*.

Jeff started racing the quarter midget (a small car, just 6 feet—183 cm—long, with an engine that generates only about 15 to 20 horsepower) when he was only five years old. He drove it on a racetrack, not on the street. In three years, he had won his first national championship with it.

His mother still wasn't very happy. She couldn't believe a motorized vehicle was less dangerous than a bike, but Jeff never got hurt driving as a child. The closest he came to any serious injury was when he fell and broke his nose at the baby-sitter's house.

Racing on four wheels was perfect for Jeff. Bickford put together a heavy schedule for him. Jeff raced every weekend, across the United States. Three years later, he won the national championship.

Jeff Gordon began racing go-karts, like this one, at the age of nine.

Other parents saw that Bickford, who owned a company that manufactured special car parts for handicapped drivers, had built most of Jeff's vehicles. They wanted him to make quarter midgets for their children, too. Jeff also started to attract fans. So Bickford had T-shirts printed up.

"Somebody would come up, give us twelve dollars, and I'd go back and grab a shirt and give it to them," Gordon said. "We were just hanging T-shirts in the back of a truck."

Jeff switched to *go-karts* at age nine and kept winning — often against drivers seven and eight years older than he was. In 1985, when he and John built a *sprint car*, Jeff had three national quarter-midget championships and four national go-kart titles. By then it was time to move on, and the sprint car was the perfect next step. The $25,000 vehicle weighed 1,300 pounds (1,590 kg) and had a 650-horsepower engine. His career was getting serious. The family moved from California to Pittsboro, Indiana, to be close to tracks where Jeff—just fourteen years old—could race. He won three times in the next two years, in Indiana, Ohio, and Illinois. Along the way, he developed the kind of business sense that would serve him well later in life.

He was still just fourteen when he walked into the offices of the Valvoline motor oil company in Indiana. He wanted the same free motor oil other racers on the sprint circuit were receiving. The Valvoline executives were surprised and amused.

One asked, "How did you get here?"

Jeff replied, "My mother drove me."

"Let me get this straight," he said. "You drive a 650-horsepower sprint car on half-mile tracks, and you had to get your mom to drive you down here?"

Bickford had put Jeff up to it. He wanted his stepson to get used to talking to sponsors. If he was going to become a big-time driver, Jeff needed to know how the business worked.

When Jeff turned sixteen, he received his USAC

Racing Levels

If you think auto racing is just for grown-ups, think again. There are many different levels of competition, and participants can begin as early as their fifth birthdays.

It all begins with go-kart racing in tiny machines that can go up to 35 mph (56 km/h). Those who do well there can graduate to the quarter-midget circuit, where drivers ages five to sixteen race on tracks one-twentieth of a mile long (80 meters) in cars that have full roll cages, for protection, and engines that are 120–150 cubic centimeters big.

The United States Auto Club (USAC) sponsors five levels of sprint car racing, with the fastest racing done in the Silver Crown Series. Sprint cars weigh up to 1,400 pounds (635 kg), and can produce nearly 800 horsepower, reach top speeds in excess of 140 mph (725 km/h), and compete on asphalt and dirt tracks.

NASCAR sponsors three different series. The Winston Cup Series is its top stock car level, with the Busch Series a step below. There is also the Craftsman Truck Series, for pickup truck drivers.

A young fan looks on as Gordon prepares for a race.

racing license. Over the next four years, in four different USAC divisions, Jeff won twenty-two

> "I said, 'This is it; this is what I want to do.'"
> —Jeff Gordon

races and logged fifty-five top five and sixty-six top-ten finishes in ninety-three starts. In 1990 Jeff was driving 815-horsepower full midget cars. That year, he became the youngest person ever to win the USAC Midget Series national championship.

One year later he captured the USAC Silver Crown national championship. Everybody in the racing business knew something about Jeff. Jeff and his family were traveling all over the country, piling up the wins. The accommodations weren't comfortable. Jeff's mother and stepfather sacrificed a lot for Jeff. Because of that, he remained humble even after he hit it big.

"We slept in pickup trucks and

made our own [auto] parts," Carol Bickford said. "That's why I think Jeff is misunderstood by people who think he was born to rich parents and had a silver spoon in his mouth." The victories were great, and Jeff was gaining plenty of experience, but one day changed his life. In the summer of 1990 Jeff showed up at a driving school in North Carolina run by former NASCAR star Buck Baker. He had never driven a full-bodied car before, but when he got behind the wheel of a stock car, he was hooked.

"I said, 'This is it; this is what I want to do,'" Jeff recalls. "The car was different from anything that I was used to. It was so big and heavy. It felt very fast but very smooth. I loved it."

Soon, he would be part of the NASCAR world. A big part.

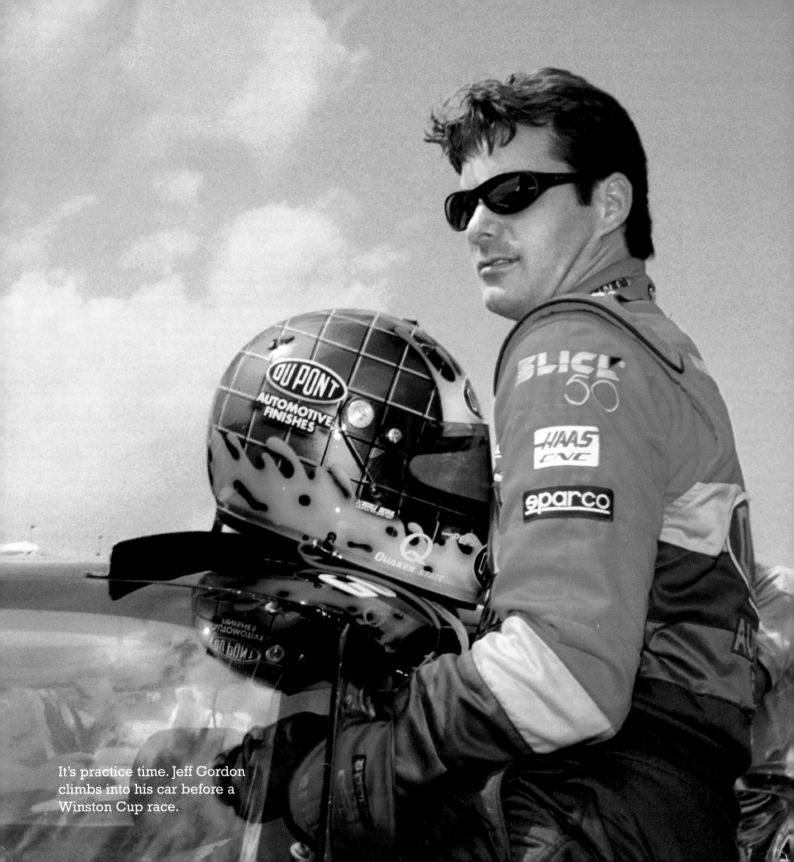

It's practice time. Jeff Gordon climbs into his car before a Winston Cup race.

CHAPTER THREE

First Success

Jeff Gordon's success began in March 1992. He was running third in a Busch Series race in Atlanta, one level below the NASCAR superstars. Busch races were usually held on Saturdays, while the NASCAR main race took place on Sunday afternoons. Just ahead were Dale Earnhardt and Harry Gant, a pair of big-name drivers. Gordon was bolting. Gordon was moving. Gordon was being watched.

Rick Hendrick, owner of the biggest, richest Winston Cup racing team and of more than seventy-five automotive dealerships across the United States, was on his way to a seat in a luxury box. He stopped long enough to watch Gordon. Gordon's crew had set the car up so that it would go faster through turns. The car allows its driver to maintain higher speeds more consistently. But it is dangerous. One bad move, one poor decision, and disaster can strike.

"I said, 'Man, that guy's gonna wreck,'" Hendrick said. "I told the people with me, 'You just can't drive a car that loose.' But the car went on to win the race. I asked who the driver was. Somebody said, 'That's that kid Gordon.'"

The fastest qualifying driver in every pre-race practice round gets the pole position to start the race, the best spot on the track.

"That kid" had moved from sprints, midgets, and karts to stock car racing. In 1991 Gordon signed with team owner Bill Davis and started competing on the Busch circuit. That year, he finished second three times and third once, with five top-fives and ten top-tens. That performance earned him the Vortex Comics Rookie of the Year award. In early 1992, when Hendrick saw Gordon hurtling around the track in his car, he was intrigued. He asked for a meeting. Gordon had impressed him. Now, he wanted to meet him. Hendrick prepared for the worst. Someone who was so successful at such a young age might be very cocky. But not Gordon.

"I was almost in a daze," Hendrick said. "Gordon had it all. It was just scary. He's good-looking, and I can't believe how well he handled himself at age twenty.

What I found was a mature young guy who was kind of humble—a little bashful. A sponsor's dream."

In May, Gordon signed with Hendrick, and a NASCAR dynasty was born. Not that Gordon wasn't capable of succeeding on his own. At that point, he had won more than 600 races during his career. But the top level of the stock car racing ladder is highly competitive. Drivers need to land big-time sponsors to help pay their expenses, which for Hendrick's three-driver team are $20 million a year. Gordon needed Hendrick, and the Hendrick team was thrilled to get Gordon.

The team grew even more pleased as the 1992 Busch Series unfolded. Gordon followed up his great debut by winning at Atlanta, and set a Busch record by capturing eleven *poles* (the best starting position in a race, determined by the fastest qualifying time). He had proved himself at that level. It was time to move ahead.

In 1993 Gordon moved on to the Winston Cup tracks, where he would drive against the best drivers in the world. Dale Earnhardt, Rusty Wallace, Bill Elliott, and the other champions weren't about to let some kid race past them. Or were they? Maybe they

> **"Gordon had it all. It was just scary. He's good-looking, and I can't believe how well he handled himself at age twenty."**
> —**Rick Hendrick**

The Winston Cup Series

Beginning in February with the Daytona 500—stock car racing's most famous event, and the sport's version of the Indy 500—and continuing through mid-November, the Winston Cup Series rules the racing world.

Hundreds of thousands of fans turn out for each event, to cheer on their favorite drivers, who can exceed 200 mph (322 km/h) in their supercharged race cars.

In 2002, there were thirty-six events; each track is at least 300 miles (483 km/h) long. Drivers spend two days qualifying for prime starting spots and then race on Sunday afternoons (there are a few Saturday-night affairs, like the Sharpie 500, in Bristol, Tennessee) for the checkered flag.

Gordon is all business behind the wheel

had no choice. Gordon proved that in his first race, the 125-mile (201-km) *qualifier* for the Daytona 500. The Daytona starts the Winston Cup season and is perhaps the most prestigious of all NASCAR races. So what did Gordon do in his debut? He won the race, of course. He also won Rookie of the Year honors, thanks to record first-year earnings of $765,000. Gordon was on his way.

Though each race has a life of its own, drivers also compete in something bigger—the Winston Cup points race. At each event, points are earned by drivers, based on where they finish. Whoever has accumulated the most points at the end of the season is crowned the Winston Cup champion.

The real fun for Gordon began in 1994, when he made his way to the winner's circle for the first (but hardly the last) time. It wasn't easy and it required a risky strategy. In May at the Coca-Cola 600 in Charlotte, North Carolina, Gordon was trailing Rusty Wallace by a few seconds when he had to make a *pit stop*. But instead of replacing all four tires on his car, which is what is usually done, Gordon just switched two. He was trying to save time and hoping that the car would still grip the road properly without a full, new set of tires. The gamble paid off. Gordon passed Wallace and won the race. When he came out of the car, he was crying for joy. And his competition was impressed. "I never thought he'd try two tires, and I'd never thought it'd work," Wallace told reporters after the race. "It was a chancy move. It was a pretty savvy move on their part."

Gordon's second Winston Cup win didn't require such a courageous move, but it was no less impressive. On August 6, just two days after his twenty-third birthday, Gordon won the Brickyard 400, the first NASCAR event ever run at the Indianapolis Motor Speedway. To do it, he had to outdrive veteran Ernie Irvan, who lost his lead when he suffered a blown right front tire with just four laps remaining. It was quite a homecoming for Gordon, who had grown up just a few miles from the Speedway.

"Indiana's my hometown," he said.

Pretty soon, he would have a new address—the winner's circle.

Yahoo! Gordon celebrates another victory by leaping on top of his number 24 Chevy.

CHAPTER FOUR

Superstardom

Jeff Gordon's 1997 campaign was a great follow-up to what had been a spectacular near miss in 1996. Gordon had won ten times in 1996 and finished just thirty-seven points behind teammate Terry Labonte in the Winston Cup standings. It wasn't a championship season, but it was a great one. And it was the perfect lead-in to the giant 1997 year.

In the first seventeen races of the 1997 Winston Cup season, Jeff Gordon won seven times. With more than forty drivers taking part in every race, Gordon's wins established him as a force to be reckoned with.

It may have been a seventeenth-place finish that was the biggest of the year. That was where Gordon ended up in the NAPA Auto Parts 500 at the Atlanta Motor Speedway. So, why was he showering crew members with champagne and celebrating? He had won his second Winston Cup points title. It hadn't been easy. It hadn't been pretty. But it was his.

Team Gordon had entered the race needing to finish eighteenth to clinch the points title. That's hardly the Gordon style. He races to win. But when Gordon crashed during the qualifying race, the strategy changed. Because his first car wasn't able to go, and his crew didn't have a whole lot of time to get the backup ready, Gordon played it safe.

When his car is hitting on all cylinders, Gordon is hard to beat.

"We didn't get conservative until Sunday morning (race day)," crew chief Ray Evernham said after the race. "We came here with every intention of winning the race with our other car. We just didn't have enough time to dial the backup car in. So, we had a meeting this morning, and I said, 'We have two strikes against us already. The ball game's at stake here, and we can't be taking any wild swings.' That's when we decided to race for the championship."

Some criticized Gordon for taking the title in less-than-spectacular fashion. But those folks conveniently forgot how often Gordon had won during the season. He captured the Daytona 500, won his first-ever *road-course* title at Watkins Glen, and finished first at the first 500-mile (805-km) race at the California Speedway. He finished out of the top twenty only five times.

"Everybody started racing at Daytona Beach with zero points, and everybody raced all year for every point he could get," said Mark Martin, who finished a close second to Gordon in the points race. "It doesn't matter when or where you got [the points]. The team with the most is champion."

If 1997 season was great, then the next year was even better. Gordon had referred to 1997 as "one of those career years." He had no idea what was ahead.

In 1998 Gordon had the kind of year that creates racing legends. He won thirteen times in thirty-three races, tying legendary driver "King" Richard Petty's modern-day mark for victories. Petty was the first NASCAR superstar, and his record was set once the circuit began keeping formal records. In the early days

After winning the 1997 Daytona 500, Gordon couldn't help thinking that even bigger victories were ahead.

of stock car racing, drivers competed in unorganized events, and results were hard to keep straight. Gordon also took his third points title, and set a NASCAR record by winning $9.3 million. Included in those thirteen triumphs were four in a row—that had never happened before in the highly competitive NASCAR world. "We like to accomplish things people tell us we can't," Gordon said. "We just show them what we can do."

The huge season gave Gordon forty wins from 1995 to 1998, an amazing figure. It also solidified his status as the sport's biggest sensation. Although more established drivers, like Dale Earnhardt and Rusty Wallace, had been racing longer, none matched Gordon's on-and-off-track appeal. His loyal fans bought the products he endorsed and

"We like to accomplish things people tell us we can't. We just show them what we can do."
—Jeff Gordon

mobbed him whenever he was out in public.

But an ugly side of Gordon's success and popularity became apparent as he continued to win. While his fans were enthusiastic and cheered for him, many other racing buffs let Gordon know how much they didn't like him. Loudly. Whenever Gordon's name was mentioned at a racetrack, there were as many boos as cheers. Some thought Gordon had too much success too quickly. Most people disagreed.

The distinctive number 24 Chevy is one of the most popular cars in all of NASCAR.

"Where does it say you have to get beat up and knocked around and maybe run out of this sport, before people think you've paid your dues?" former NASCAR star Darrell Waltrip said. "If you're good, you're good. Why should it matter how or when you got here? I can't buy into that."

> "If you're good, you're good. Why should it matter how or when you got here? I can't buy into that."
> —Darrell Waltrip

Still, those who disliked Gordon felt he had it all—a great team, good looks, and lots of money. So they tried to bring him down.

"When the boos first started, I didn't understand," Gordon says. "I guess it hurt my feelings a little bit. But then I decided, 'Aw, what the heck, they're race fans and they can boo if they want to.' In a way, I guess it's a compliment because fans generally only boo athletes who win a lot."

Gordon *was* winning a lot. And he *was* getting booed. But everything was fine in Gordon's world—for the time being. The next two years would test his driving ability, his tact, and maturity. It would be tough, but Gordon would pass the test.

Jeff Gordon doesn't just drive—he is always looking for ways to make his car run faster.

CHAPTER FIVE
The "Slump"

*J*eff Gordon had it all. He was a three-time Winston Cup points champion before his thirtieth birthday. He had won more money in a season than anybody else in history. Life was good. Then the trouble began.

On September 28, 1999, Gordon's longtime crew chief, Ray Evernham, left the Rainbow Warriors to become the owner of Bill Elliott's and Casey Atwood's racing teams. The man who had been with Gordon from the beginning and had helped him go from a NASCAR newcomer to a champion was gone. Gordon's fans worried. Those who rooted against number 24 each week were thrilled. Was this the end of an era?

There was good reason for concern. The 1999 season hadn't gone so well for Gordon. Even though he would win seven races, take home $5.8 million in prize money, and finish sixth in the Winston Cup standings, he was a long way from what he had accomplished in 1998. Now, with Evernham gone, many believed Gordon would fall even farther from the NASCAR summit. Evernham, however, wasn't one of them.

"Jeff has been ready to be a leader for some time," he said. "Jeff and I first got together when he was eighteen. My role was to be the mentor, and he was the student. But he doesn't need a mentor anymore."

The immediate impact of Evernham's departure wasn't so bad. Team owner Rick

In 1999, Gordon's longtime crew chief and mentor, Ray Evernham, left to form his own team.

Hendrick named Brian Whitesell the new crew chief. Whitesell had been with Gordon since 1992 and had worked his way to a position of influence and considerable responsibility within the team. Gordon won his first two races—in Martinsville, Virginia, and Charlotte, North Carolina—with Whitesell running the show.

But that success didn't continue. Gordon's average finish in the season's final five races was sixteenth. Worse, at the end of the year, five members of his pit crew left to sign with Dale Jarrett, another NASCAR driver and a top Gordon rival. Things were not looking very good.

So Gordon took control. When Whitesell said he would be happier in another role with the team, Gordon let him leave his post. "Brian wasn't that happy being the crew chief," Gordon said. "He's always been more comfortable with managing the big picture than standing on top of the box and making the calls."

Whitesell was happy, but Gordon still needed a new crew chief. He turned to Robbie Loomis, who had been handling the same job for John Andretti, another NASCAR competitor. It was an easy choice, since Evernham had said many good things

"Jeff and I first got together when he was eighteen. My role was to be the mentor, and he was the student. But he doesn't need a mentor anymore."

—Ray Evernham

Gordon chose Robbie Loomis (left) to take over as crew chief and to bring him back to the Winner's Circle.

about Loomis before leaving. "Jeff didn't need a crew chief to be the leader of the team," Evernham said. "He just needed someone who believed in him. And Robbie thought that Jeff was the best driver in the world."

By the time the 2000 season began, the Gordon team had fourteen new members, including a fresh chief. The cars, a pair of updated Monte Carlos, were also new. Gordon thought the transition would be quick, but it wasn't. Gordon's average finish in the first fourteen races was fifteenth. He could forget about a run at the points championship. Gordon was just trying to get comfortable.

When Gordon finished fourth at Martinsville in early April, he sounded thrilled. Thrilled with fourth?

"Today was like a win for us," he said. "It was a great effort all around. We got the most out of the car. The previous races this year, we haven't."

Gordon's fans wondered whether it was all Loomis's fault. After all, the driver hadn't changed, but the crew had. Still, Gordon didn't panic, even when he finished thirty-second at the MBNA Platinum 400 in Dover, Delaware, in early June. He was too good a driver to doubt himself. And he had some great competition all around him.

No driver does it alone. Here, Gordon's pit crew adds fuel and changes tires on the number 24 Chevy.

Nobody had said it would be easy. "I think one of the things that I'm very proud of is that even though we've struggled a little bit, my guys have been up," he said. "They haven't gotten down. They haven't started blaming or pointing fingers at one another. They knew with time it would come, with hard work and dedication it would come. There's never been any doubt in my mind if we were patient and if we stuck together and didn't get down on ourselves and lose confidence, we could get back to Victory Lane."

"There's never been any doubt in my mind if we were patient and if we stuck together and didn't get down on ourselves and lose confidence, we could get back to Victory Lane."
— **Jeff Gordon**

That happened in September, when Gordon won the Chevrolet 400 in Richmond. It was his fifty-second Winston Cup career win, and a signal that good things were ahead. Gordon had ten top-ten finishes in his final eleven races in 2000. He finished the year with three wins, $3 million in prize money, and a ninth-place points finish. Best of all, he and Loomis had weathered a minor slump and seemed ready to make a run back to the top in 2001.

"Late in the 2000 season, because I had been around Jeff for a while, I started to understand what adjustments needed to be made just by how forcefully Jeff would say something over the (car) radio," Loomis said. "We finally learned each other's language."

In 2001 that talk would turn to winning—often.

Success returned in 2000 when Gordon broke out of his slump.

Sealed with a kiss. Gordon celebrates his
win at the Sharpie 500 by kissing the trophy.

CHAPTER SIX
Coming Back with a Vengeance

"We're back!" Jeff Gordon said as his car roared first across the finish line at the UAW-DaimlerChrysler 400 in Las Vegas.

With those simple words, Gordon let the Winston Cup circuit know that 2001 was going to be his year.

Two weeks after finishing a dismal thirtieth at Daytona, in the first race of the year, Gordon had taken the checkered flag. Though he was racing with a heavy heart—like all NASCAR drivers—due to the tragic death of Dale Earnhardt at Daytona, Gordon and his team were rolling again. The win in Las Vegas showed just how much they had grown together since their fresh start a year before.

Thanks to small adjustments made during Gordon's pit stops, the Rainbow machine ran faster as the race went on. By the time it was over, Gordon had moved from the back of the field to win for the first time—though certainly not the last—in 2001.

"We did not have the best car at the beginning of that race, but we did at the end," Gordon said when the year was over. "After we won, the team realized this could be a special season."

It sure was. Before it was over, Gordon had made a loud and clear move back to the top of the Winston Cup circuit. Even though he faded somewhat during the second half

Dale Earnhardt

Until his untimely death at the 2001 Daytona 500, Earnhardt was NASCAR's "Intimidator." He dressed in black. His number 3 Dodge was black. And he drove like the old-style black-hat bad guys of the Wild West. He'd bump you. He'd ride your bumper. He'd do anything to win. But when it was over, Earnhardt would shake your hand, say, "Good race," and get ready to do it all over again the next week.

Earnhardt won seven Winston Cup points titles, and finished second three times. Although he struggled somewhat during the early 1990s, he had a comeback later in the decade. Earnhardt entered the twenty-first century as one of NASCAR's most successful and popular drivers. His legions of fans appreciated Earnhardt's courage, and he remains incredibly popular, despite his death in Daytona. His son, Dale Earnhardt, Jr., stayed in the sport after his father's death, and is now one of NASCAR's biggest and most marketable stars.

of the season, he still won enough to take the points title and a record $10.9 million. The money was nice. So was the title. But the biggest reward of the season was that he had returned to the top. And he had returned with a new crew chief.

There had always been whispers among the NASCAR community that Gordon had been winning because of Evernham. Some viewed him as a puppet of a great tutor, capable only of doing what he was told. Evernham and his crew had put together a great car every week, and then told Gordon how to drive it. The 2001 championship showed that maybe, just maybe, Gordon was winning because he knew what he was doing. After all, he had been a dominant driver at every level he raced at before meeting Evernham. Now he was on top without him.

"Jeff has the ability to see things on the racetrack in slow motion," Whitesell said. "His eye-to-hand coordination is just unbelievable."

Gordon won the 2001 title with a big first half of the season. Three months after his win in Las Vegas, Nevada, Gordon captured the MBNA Platinum 400 in Dover, Delaware, where he led for 381 of the 400 laps. The next week, he won again,

Gordon gets the checkered flag, this time for winning the 2002 Gatorade 125 at Daytona International Speedway.

this time in Michigan. He would win twice more, at Watkins Glen, New York, and in Kansas City, Missouri. He finished with a 349-point lead over second-place finisher Tony Stewart. It wasn't as impressive a season as 1998 had been, but first place is first place.

Jeff Gordon gets ready for work by climbing into his car before taking a qualifying run.

"When you win a lot of races and have won championships, even if you have a bad year, you know what it takes to get [back] to the top," Gordon said.

As the 2002 season dawned, everybody wanted to know what Gordon could do for an encore. But Gordon wasn't concerned with playing "Can You Top This?" against himself. He wanted to keep driving hard and to keep winning. He had turned thirty during the 2001 season and was entering what many considered to be the best part of a racer's life.

"I feel like I'm getting to be a better driver every day," he said. "I'm just starting to come into my prime."

That's scary news for the rest of the Winston Cup drivers. While they try to get better, the lead dog is improving, too. Gordon and Loomis are bound to work together even more effi-

Gordon made it back to the top of the NASCAR standings in 2001, winning the Winston Cup points championship.

"Jeff has the ability to see things on the racetrack in slow motion," Whitesell said. "His eye-to-hand coordination is just unbelievable."
—Brian Whitesell

ciently. And by coming back from a pair of tough seasons to win the points championship, Gordon has learned about fighting back. It was the first time he had done it during his racing career, and it had worked out well. Gordon had faced the criticism and responded the best way he knew how—by

Gordon was all smiles in 2001, as he roared to five wins and nearly
$11 million in prize money.

Jeff Gordon in the lead again!

winning. In 2002 Gordon also became the co-owner of Jimmie Johnson's number 48 car. Johnson is one of the best younger drivers on the NASCAR circuit.

The 2000 season couldn't bring him down. His spirits remained high, and he loved what he was doing.

"You have to enjoy life to its fullest," Gordon said. "And I have no regrets. I've been blessed and have enjoyed my life very, very much. So, no matter what happens, I'll always say that I've had a wonderful life."

Indeed he has. And things are getting better all the time.

Stats — Jeff Gordon

Born:	August 4, 1971	**Birthplace:**	Vallejo, California	
Height:	5'8"	**Weight:**	150	
Sponsor:	DuPont	**Car:**	#24 Chevrolet	

2002 TOTALS

Starts	Average Start	Provisionals Used	Average Finish	Points	Laps Complete	Winnings
36	12.6	1	14.0	4607	95.3%	$4,899,324

No.	Race	Start	Finish	Points	Standing Pos.	Laps/Total	Winnings	Status
1	Daytona 500	3	9	143	9	200/200	$289,674	Running
2	Subway 400	33	7	146	4	393/393	$104,238	Running
3	UAW-DaimlerChrysler 400	13	17	112	7	267/267	$116,653	Running
4	MBNA America 500	19	16	115	11	325/325	$96,478	Running
5	Carolina Dodge Dealers 400	2	9	148	6	293/293	$106,663	Running
6	Food City	1	31	75	10	480/500	$117,418	Running
7	Samsung/RadioShack 500	26	2	170	6	334/334	$296,478	Running
8	Virginia 500	1	23	99	8	498/500	$107,003	Running
9	Aaron's 499	10	4	160	7	188/188	$143,003	Running
10	NAPA Auto Parts 500	17	16	115	7	249/250	$110,078	Running
11	Pontiac Excitement 400	4	7	146	6	400/400	$99,403	Running
12	Coca-Cola Racing Family 600	16	5	155	4	400/400	$144,928	Running
13	MBNA Platinum 400	9	6	155	3	400/400	$116,558	Running
14	Pocono 500	3	5	160	3	200/200	$125,003	Running
15	Sirius Satellite Radio 400	24	5	155	3	200/200	$112,028	Running
16	Dodge/Save Mart 350	4	37	62	3	103/110	$110,368	Running
17	Pepsi 400	3	22	102	3	159/160	$110,578	Running
18	Tropicana 400	15	2	170	4	267/267	$180,268	Running
19	New England 300	11	29	76	5	300/300	$97,028	Running
20	Pennsylvania 500	28	12	127	4	175/175	$93,903	Running
21	Brickyard 400	21	6	150	4	160/160	$204,728	Running
22	Sirius Satellite Radio at The Glen	23	22	97	5	90/90	$91,928	Running
23	Pepsi 400 presented by Farmer Jack	19	19	106	5	200/200	$96,918	Running
24	Sharpie 500	1	1	185	3	500/500	$245,543	Running
25	Mountain Dew Southern 500	3	1	185	2	367/367	$212,183	Running
26	Chevy Monte Carlo 400	10	40	43	4	84/400	$92,000	Engine
27	New Hampshire 300	21	14	121	5	207/207	$101,803	Running
28	MBNA All-American Heroes 400	24	37	52	5	319/400	$97,503	Accident
29	Protection One 400	10	1	185	4	267/267	$217,928	Running
30	EA SPORTS 500	4	42	42	7	125/188	$107,258	Engine
31	UAW-GM Quality 500	8	4	160	6	334/334	$125,778	Running
32	Old Dominion 500	2	36	55	6	497/500	$90,753	Running
33	NAPA 500	7	6	155	7	248/248	$124,978	Running
34	Pop Secret Microwave Popcorn 400	18	5	155	7	393/393	$106,713	Running
35	Checker Auto Parts 500 Presented by Penzoil	4	3	170	6	312/312	$152,328	Running
36	Ford 400	37	5	155	4	267/267	$152,278	Running

Figures compiled from www.nascar.com.

GLOSSARY

go-kart—A compact car, driven by smaller competitors on short tracks at speeds well below full-sized race cars, usually topping out at 30 to 35 mph (48–56 km/h).

NASCAR—The abbreviation for National Association for Stock Car Auto Racing.

pit stop—A stop made by a race car driver in a special off-track areas, usually to refuel and change tires, but also for more serious repairs.

poles—The spot in the starting lineup of cars given to the driver who has posted the fastest qualifying time.

qualifier—A race held to determine who will compete in a later, more important event. The number of drivers who will qualify varies, depending on the number of cars allowed in the field and how many drivers are already eligible to compete without qualifying.

quarter midget—A race car for drivers ages five to sixteen which has a full four-wheel independent suspension, a full roll cage for protection and 120- to 150-cubic-centimeter engines. Drivers compete on tracks 1/20th of a mile (80 m) long.

road course—A race track that is not contained in an oval. It can take any shape and replicates a road's unpredictable twists and turns.

sprint car—A 12- to 14-foot (3.7–4.3-m) long, 1,200-pound (544-kg) vehicle that reaches speeds in excess of 140 mph (225 km/h) and generates up to 800 horsepower. Sprint car races are held throughout the country on dirt and asphalt tracks.

stock car—A race car based on a major manufacturer's "stock" body type. It is then outfitted to compete at speeds of more than 200 mph (322 km/h), but its look comes close to a car that can be seen in a car dealer's showroom.

Winston Cup—The series of races held throughout the year that determine the annual NASCAR points champion. Racers compete for points in each race, with a better finish guaranteeing more points. Whoever ends the year with the most points is declared the Winston Cup champion.

FIND OUT MORE

Web Sites
NASCAR Official Site
http://www.nascar.com

Jeff Gordon Official Site
http://www.jeffgordon.com

Books

Garfield, Ken. *Jeff Gordon: Rewriting the Record Book*. New York: Sports Publishing Inc., 2001.

Johnstone, Michael. *NASCAR*. Minneapolis, MN: First Avenue Editions, 2002.

MacNow, Glen. *Jeff Gordon*. Berkeley Heights, NJ: Enslow Publishers, Inc. 2001.

Mooney, Loren, Scott Gramling, and Sherie Holder. *A Kid's Guide to NASCAR*. New York: Sports Illustrated for Kids, 1999.

⭐ *Jeff Gordon*

INDEX

Page numbers in **boldface** are illustrations.

PHOTO CREDITS